Camels
IN NEVADA

by Douglas McDonald

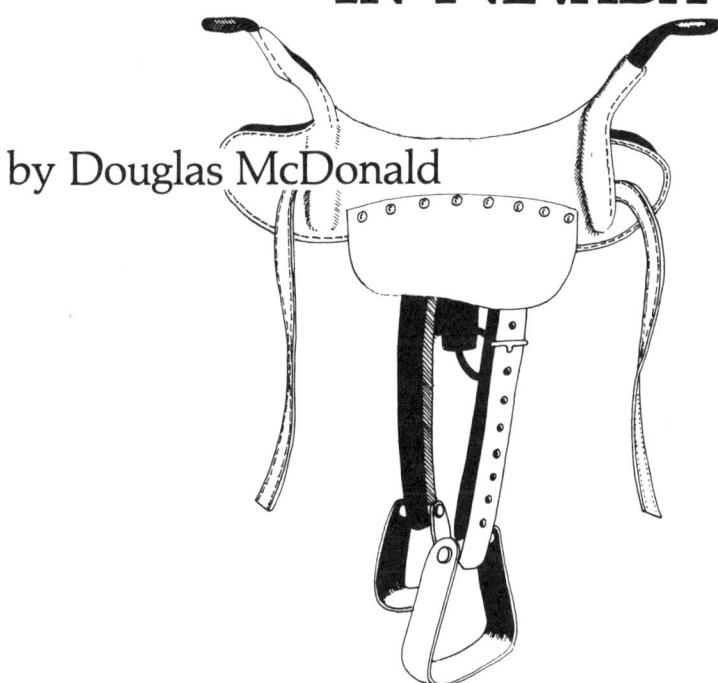

Nevada Publications
Box 15444
Las Vegas, Nevada

Copyright ©1983 by Douglas McDonald. All rights reserved.
Printed in the USA. ISBN 0-913814-56-3.

Camels
IN NEVADA

Not long after midnight on a moonless night in September 1861, two burly Comstock miners were happily spending their pay in a wood-frame saloon on the outskirts of Virginia City. They had imbibed freely before their dwindling funds prompted the beginning of their journey home. The men had walked just a few feet when the silhouette of a man on a huge hump-backed animal appeared in the night's blackness. As distinctive camel groans echoed down the street, one of the miners stood transfixed with his mouth gaping. The other hurriedly dropped to his knees, and while crossing himself, muttered: "Sweet Jesus! 'Tis the resurrection itself."

This unusual legend points to a very early use of camels in Nevada, but actually the beasts had been part of western transportation since 1835. In that year the first serious campaign to use camels was first put forward when Major George H. Crossman began arguing for the U.S. government to fund a military experiment using these animals in the desert Southwest. Though the American West was nothing like the sandy wastes of Egypt and Arabia, he still felt that in some areas of the Southwest the camel could definitely prove useful.

For several years Major Crossman promoted his idea, aided by contemporary newspapers which called the unmapped regions of the West the "Great American Desert." Since "desert" and "camels" fit well together in the public's eye, support for his proposal gradually developed. Finally he won the backing of Senator Jefferson Davis, who in 1851 chaired the Senate Committee on Military Affairs.

Davis also had ulterior motives. Through the 1850's, many southerners believed that war between the North and the South was inevitable. Davis' support of the camel plan was eminently logical, for it would encourage transportation between the southern states and the newly discovered goldfields of California.

Davis sought a $30,000 appropriation to import 30 camels, 20 dromedaries, and ten Arab handlers for his southwestern military experiment. However, his Senate colleagues greeted the proposal with laughter and derision, defeating it 24 to 19.

In 1852 Senator Shields of Illinois proposed a similiar bill for funds to import camels. Since Davis' groundwork had convinced several Senators of the feasibility of the measure, it passed 26 to 16. But the House of Representatives had no staunch supporters to lobby for its passage, and so the camel-funding idea again went down to defeat.

In 1853-54 similiar amendments were added to the appropriations bill for the U.S. Army. Though defeated both years, the public in general and important military men began to support the idea. Lectures, military

Dromedaries were especially noted for their speed and endurance. Gwinn H. Heap, in trying to convince the U.S. government of the usefulness of camels, wrote in 1854: "I saw a party of Arabs, mounted on dromedaries, arrive in Tunis in four days from Tripoli, a distance of 600 miles."

reports, and a best-selling novel, *The Camel Hunt*, all contributed to a greater awareness of camels.

The American Camel Company was incorporated in New York in 1854 to import camels for use in transportation "over the deserts lying between the Mississippi and the Pacific Ocean." It never did obtain any animals, but by 1855 Congress appropriated $30,000 with which to purchase camels, enormously pleasing Jefferson Davis, who had since become Secretary of War.

Army Major Henry C. Wayne and Lieutenant David D. Porter, a 42-year old Naval officer, were placed in joint command of the storeship *U.S.S. Supply* and ordered to sail to North Africa on a camel buying trip. Wayne had previously studied the camel at great length, writing a report in 1853 entitled "General Remarks on the Use of Camels and Dromedaries for Transportation and Military Purposes..." That document had so pleased Davis that when the time came to secure the animals for the government, Wayne was promised the job.

The *Supply* was remodeled to enable it to transport camels before she set sail for the Mediterranean. At Tunis, the expedition purchased a camel before learning that a special permit had to be obtained to export it. Fortunately Mohammed Pasha, the Bey of Tunis, not only agreed to the permit but generously gave the Americans two camels from his own stable.

"The camel's haughty manner and disdainful looks stem from the fact that he alone knows the 100th name of Allah, while man knows but 99." (Old Islamic saying.)

The ship then sailed to Malta and Smyrna, where the officers learned that most of the dromedaries there had been led away to battle in the Crimean War. Porter and Wayne eventually visited the Crimea to determine if the animals fared well in war. They soon saw how the camel performed as 1,000 soldiers, loaded two to an animal, often covered 70 miles in 12 hours. They almost exclusively used the one-humped Arabian camel, or dromedary, convincing the officers to limit future purchases to that species.

By the time the *Supply* was ready to sail for home, the expedition had acquired 31 Arabian camels and two Bactrians. Additionally, two Arabs, an Armenian, and two Turkish saddle makers also accompanied the camels to America. On May 13, 1856, the animals were landed at Indianola, Texas. Their difference from horses and mules was soon made evident when a 200-foot corral, constructed of prickly pear, was built to house them. Other animals would stay clear of the thorny fence but the camels soon ate it up!

Since less than half of the $30,000 appropriation had been spent so far, the *Supply* was ordered back for more animals as Porter and Wayne had hoped. On February 10, 1857, the ship landed 41 more camels on the Texas coast, along with eight men who would work with the animals. These included Hadji Ali and George Caralambo, who would forever after be known as "Hi Jolly" and "Greek George."

Meanwhile Major Wayne, who had stayed in Texas, had moved the first group of camels to Camp Verde, north of San Antonio. Although it was an active military post, he ordered built a special khan, or camel corral, to

Mid-Eastern specifications. Here Army soldiers were taught how to pack and ride camels from the native handlers. Unfortunately the praise written about the beasts could never convince most enlisted men to like camels, and some soldiers even developed a distinct hatred for them.

Americans found the camels to be quite smelly; the males proved to be especially dangerous as well. Army personnel never seemed to adapt to riding camel saddles, growing "seasick" from their rotating motion. Inexperienced soldiers often packed the camels wrong, thus causing sores which put the animal out of commission until they were healed. Horses and mules were scared witless by the sight and smell of camels and their approach often stampeded a Cavalry troop.

It is easy to see why so many camels ended their military service by "escaping," usually with the assistance of the very men assigned to guard them. A few others were callously killed, while still more were "mistakenly" shot at night by disgruntled sentries.

In January 1857, John B. Floyd became Secretary of War. Major Wayne was reassigned, and the command of the camel outfit was transferred to former Navy Lt. Edward F. Beale. His instructions were to use them to establish a wagon road from Fort Defiance, New Mexico, westward to the lower Colorado River.

On June 25 Beale with his party and 25 camels set out for Ft. Defiance. They took some time settling into trail routine but eventually they passed safely through El Paso, Albuquerque and on to Ft. Defiance. By September

This undated painting by Ernest Narjot of a camel train in the Southwest probably portrays Lt. Beale's 1857 expedition from Ft. Defiance to the Colorado River.

5 the party passed near present Holbrook, Arizona, where the terrain became exceedingly rough. It was very difficult to locate water; the mules suffered so badly that scouts were constantly sent ahead mounted on dromedaries. When there was no choice to move onward except down a steep volcanic descent, a camel led the way to give confidence to the other animals. Finally, after becoming lost once and delayed several times, the party reached the Colorado River on October 17. Two days later, after Beale purchased fresh melons from the local Mohave Indians, the camels further proved their usefulness by calmly and safely swimming across the river. When the rest of the party followed, two horses and 10 mules panicked and were drowned.

From that river crossing just north of Needles, California, the party split into two groups with the majority turning westward to Fort Tejon. Beale took two camels and a few of the men to Los Angeles where he put on an Arabian show with Hi Jolly riding the camel Tuili, both garbed in native dress, before joining the others at Fort Tejon.

While the camels were stationed at the fort, several were sent to a camp high in the Sierra Nevada, where they adapted very well to the deep snow. In fact, when a wagon loaded with provisions for Fort Tejon became snowbound, and six mules could not budge it, a party of camels easily pulled it out of the drift.

The camels proved so effective that Secretary of War Floyd recommended to Congress that an additional thousand be purchased for the Army. Everyone ignored his idea, though Floyd renewed his request annually until the advent of the Civil War, with both he and Beale constantly relating tales of the camels' achievements to anyone who would listen.

During 1857-58 a group of camels remained based at Ft. Tejon. They packed supplies for the fort, even carrying mail for a brief period, though generally they saw little use. In 1861 their old friend, Edward Beale, was appointed Surveyor General of California and Nevada. As arrangements had already been made to survey the California-Nevada boundary from the Colorado River to Lake Tahoe, Beale enthusiastically endorsed the use of camels for this expedition.

In February 1861 the party of 14 men, three horses, three camels, and 22 mules set off from a site near Needles and headed north. After traveling nearly 60 days, the party eventually terminated the project near Visalia, again demonstrating the feasibility of using camels in nearly every sort of terrain.

The year 1861 also saw the war start between the Union and the Confederacy. The Quartermaster at Fort Tejon had previously allocated 20 camels to Beale's use, which had been managed so well that when they were turned in during June their number had increased to 31 animals, all in excellent shape.

These camels were transferred to Camp Fitzgerald in Los Angeles where an effort was again made to utilize them. A 300 mile long dromedary ex-

Camel Artillery

In the Mid-East camels were even used as mobile gun platforms for light artillery. Known as Zembourek, this Persian fighting force consisted of two camels and three men to each gun. Two soldiers and half of the ammunition and equipment traveled on one camel while the third man rode with the gun and the remainder of the equipment on a second animal. The piece could be discharged directly from the camel's back, but it was usually dismounted and fired from its combination saddle-carriage.

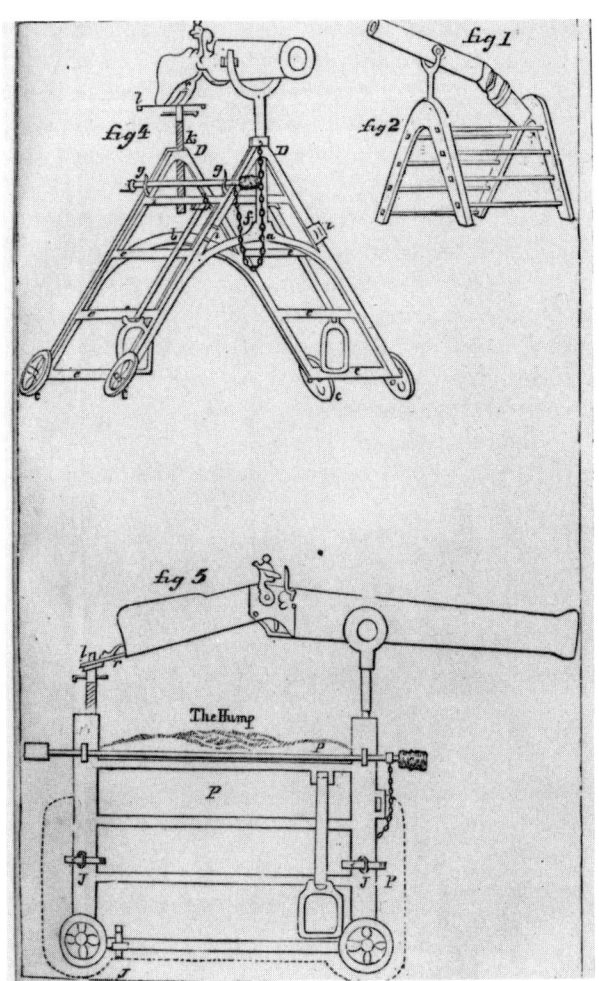
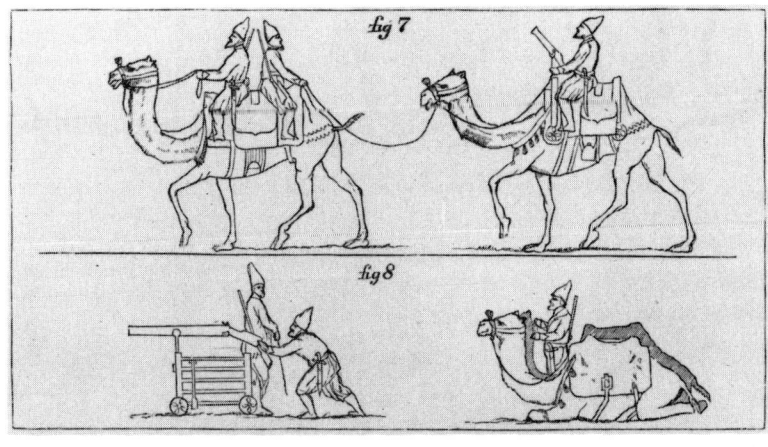

press was started between Los Angeles and Fort Mohave, Arizona, though it was abandoned after only a few trips, one of which ended in the death of the camel. In 1862 some camels hauled freight between San Pedro and Los Angeles, then in the following year another camel express was started from San Pedro to Tucson. Between these short-lived experiments the camels for the most part spent their days in idleness.

Late in 1863 the Army decided that they had no further use for camels. The Union owned only 37 as Confederates in Texas had captured 54 others at the onset of the war. The Union's camels were trailed north to San Francisco Bay, arriving in Benicia on January 17, 1864. A little more than a month later, on February 26, they were sold at public auction to Samuel McLeneghan, who had worked with the animals for several years as a government employee.

While the saga of "Uncle Sam's Camel Corps" had ended, camels of a different sort began to make an indelible mark on the Far West. Five years

One of the more unusual camels brought to the U.S. by the Army was a Tuili, or half-breed cross between a Bactrian and an Arabian. Later this animal was used in Nevada where its name was modified to "Tule" after the predominant reeds which grow near desert water sources.

earlier, on May 23, 1859, John Ager and nine other Downieville, California residents chartered the California and Utah Camel Association. Its purpose was "the introduction, and employment of the Camel on the Pacific Coast," but the backers failed to pursue the matter further.

Then a few weeks later the enormous silver deposit of the Comstock Lode was discovered in what was then western Utah Territory, and Virginia City was founded. As silver was much more complex to refine than gold, one item needed in quantity was salt, which was believed to be an agent to help roast the ore during the milling process. Long mule trains soon snaked their way over the Sierra Nevada, bringing salt where at Virginia City it fetched the enormous price of $120 per ton.

Otto Esche, a German businessman living in San Francisco, had heard much of the packing ability of the camels used in the Army experiments. He figured that since a camel could carry more than twice the load of a mule, he would profit from a camel train service to the Comstock Lode.

In the spring of 1860 Esche secured financial partners, chartered the schooner *Caroline E. Foote*, and sailed to Siberia. By June 1 he had traveled to Mongolia's Amur River region where he purchased 32 Bactrian camels. He lost 17 while driving them to the port but he was still able to load the rest and ship them off to California, where they arrived in San Francisco on July 25, 1860. Two died soon after arrival. Three others auctioned on October 10 brought such low prices that the remaining ten camels were removed from the sale. They were then consigned to Julius Bandmann, who pastured them in San Francisco during the next year.

Meanwhile, Esche patiently combed the Amur region searching for more good Bactrians, finally collecting nearly 60 animals and hiring two camel handlers, Ali and Assan. On September 10, 1861 the *Caroline E. Foote* returned to the Siberian port of Nicolaessky, where a week later the bark *Dollart* also arrived to unload cargo. Esche hired the second vessel as well, a ship five times larger than the schooner. When the *Caroline E. Foote* sailed for California she was carrying ten Bactrians; the *Dollart* was loaded with 44 of them.

The *Caroline E. Foote* landed in San Francisco on November 15, 1861 with all ten of her camels healthy. Unfortunately, the captain of the *Dollart* was so negligent that when his ship arrived in San Francisco on February 26, 1862, all but 20 animals had perished. Esche himself had been injured while traveling on the *Dollart* and he immediately filed suit against her captain, J. H. C. Muggenborg, for the loss of 24 camels.

Just two months before the *Caroline E. Foote* landed in San Francisco, Julius Bandmann believed that he had learned enough about Esche's first ten camels that he should be able to turn a profit with them. He, too, realized that the easiest cargo to carry would be salt for the Nevada silver reduction mills, so on speculation he drove nine of the camels to Virginia City in September, 1861.

When the first group of camels was sent from California to Nevada late in 1861, artist Edward Vischer accompanied the caravan. The trail they followed was known as the Big Trees Route for the giant redwoods growing in the vicinity. Here the train passes through Mammoth Grove on its way to Genoa, Carson City, and Virginia City.

TREE-ROUTE, passing through the MAMMOTH GROVE (Sept. 1860).

His route passed through Angels Camp, over Ebbetts Pass, and into Hope Valley, then turned north through Genoa and Carson City before he reached the Comstock. Sketches made by artist Edward Vischer, who accompanied the caravan, show that the camels were driven unladen and not roped together, perhaps because Bandmann was simply ferrying them to Nevada to be sold. At any rate in Virginia City the Chevalier brothers, Marius and Louis, purchased all nine animals, paying about $250 apiece.

The brothers owned a ranch on the Carson River between Dayton and Fort Churchill. Louis, a veteran of the French Army in North Africa, was keenly aware of the potential profit that might be made with these animals in the freight business.

54. DESCENT TO CARSON VALLEY.
Bactrian Camels brought over the Sierra Nevada. Encampment in sight of the Desert.

Bandmann continued to accompany the camels when they were next sent to a salt marsh "near Walker River." This was most probably the Columbus Salt Marsh although after mid-1862 the larger deposits at Rhodes Salt Marsh were the primary source of the camels' cargo. Bancroft's 1863 map of Nevada Territory shows a "camel trail" leading northwest from Rhodes Salt Marsh along the east shore of Walker Lake past Fort Churchill to Virginia City.

The first camels were only packed with about 500 pounds of salt, on account of the high altitude and rugged country, yet at the prevailing price of $120 per ton in Virginia City the caravan still yielded a profit of about $250 on each ten day trip.

To further cut costs, Mexican handlers were hired to accompany the camel trains, but these men unfortunately knew little about proper care for the animals. Early in January, 1863 the *Washoe Times* observed that of the seven camels then regularly plying between the salt marshes and Virginia City, "...some are poor, while their backs are raw and bloody from the effects of careless packing."

Soon additional salt deposits were discovered much closer to Virginia City. With increased competition from large freight wagons, the price of

PICTURE FOLLOWING PAGES: *Only one photograph is presently known which shows a camel in Nevada in the 19th century. Probably taken in the late 1860's during a parade in front of Carson City's Arlington House, this unique view shows two unidentified riders mounted on a Bactrian camel. The animal is possibly Tuili, known locally as "Old Tule," and the rider dressed in native garb may well be Hi Jolly.*

Vischer's sketches were published in 1862, documenting the first time camels had crossed the Sierra Nevada mountains. Although the Bactrians which Julius Bandmann was ferrying to Virginia City had been raised in China, their first glimpse of arid Nevada Territory probably reminded them of home.

salt fell to as low as $80 per ton, yet some camel trains still packed it from flats near Sand Springs (east of present Fallon) and also from a field north of modern Fernley. The Virginia City *Evening Bulletin* of September 23, 1863 states that "A train of camels is running from the Humboldt salt mines to this city, packing salt for the Humboldt Salt Company. Each camel is able to pack from 800 to 1,000 pounds." Obviously, to counteract the reduced price salt was bringing, the camels' loads were increased in size.

All the while Julius Bandmann worked out of San Francisco, where he had been located after accompanying the first camel train from the Columbus Salt Marsh to Virginia City in 1861. When Otto Esche's two ships, the *Dollart* and the *Caroline F. Foote*, returned from the Orient with additional Bactrians, all were put in Bandmann's care. Some died but still others were born so that when 23 camels were sold to Frank Laumeister for use in British Columbia there were still eight remaining in Bandmann's pastures. Seven additional camels were born prior to March 1864 when the last 15 of Otto Esche's Bactrians were sold to the Chevalier's and transported to Nevada.

The month before, on February 26, the U.S. Army sold their remaining 34 camels at public auction, the last vestiges of their "Camel Corps." All animals were purchased at Benicia by Samuel McLeneghan, who then

resold three to a rancher named Riley in Sacramento. McLeneghan kept 31 camels on his Sonoma County ranch until April 2, when he drove ten to Sacramento. He wished to begin a freight line in the Humboldt County area of Nevada; to raise money for the venture a "Great Dromedary Race" was scheduled at the local fairgrounds.

On April 7 about a thousand people gathered to watch the event, although no organized race was actually held. Instead, six camels were first driven riderless around the half-mile track. Then all ten together, with a McLenaghan employee named O. W. Dealing mounted on one, repeated the process. Dealing hurriedly got off his camel midway around the track as he thought he would momentarily become violently ill. He finished the "race" mounted on a mule. The Sacramento *Daily Union* later remarked that "a drove of cattle driven around the course would be a good example of this 'race.'"

Not only was there no real race that day, McLeneghan was also cheated out of most of the money raised. He and the camels did start out for Nevada the following day but at Marysville they again stopped to put on another "race." A third such event was probably held at nearby Nevada City for the Gold Hill *News* reported, "At the dromedary race in Nevada, $9.50 was taken in admission and the show was compelled to pay $11 for a license." Thoroughly disgusted, McLeneghan and his camels then returned to Sacramento, although on April 18 the ten dromedaries were sent to Virginia City by Greenwood & Co., each animal carrying about 400 pounds of freight. In partnership with his half-brother, a man named LaFlamme, McLeneghan acquired a sturdy stone barn and corral in Dayton, Nevada, which had been constructed by George Leslie, to use in stabling the animals.

Along with the camels purchased at Benicia, McLeneghan also obtained the services of one of the original camel handlers, Hi Jolly. Although very little is known about him, tales of his days in Nevada have passed down through the years. One concerns the time that he and Joe Plato, a pioneer miner on the Comstock, rode two camels to San Francisco in search of a "woman of the evening" to whom Plato had deeded a seemingly worthless mining claim. In reality it contained a pay streak but she had already heard of the mine's true value, forcing Plato to marry her to get the deed back. The three of them are said to have made the honeymoon trip back to the Comstock riding the camels.

Another story relates how Hi Jolly was bilked by a Chinaman who sold him a poke containing $65 worth of gold dust. A few days later he took the poke to an assayer, intending to have the dust melted into a more convenient ingot, but was handed a tiny bar worth only $48. It seems the Chinaman had salted the dust, picked out Hi Jolly as a sucker, and skipped the country soon after the sale had been completed. But no matter what befell the patient Hi Jolly, he was always found somewhere near his unusual charges.

Throughout 1864 several camel pack trains used various means to turn a dollar. The salt prices had dropped so greatly that it was only a marginally profitable cargo, but at the same time rich silver veins were struck in the Reese River district. The first camel pack train to that area, consisting of Bactrians owned by the Chevaliers, arrived in the newly founded city of Austin on August 26, 1864. The *Reese River Reveille* commented, "The animal is not ornamental, but apparently useful." It is likely that McLeneghan and LaFlamme's dromedaries were also used for at least one run to Austin, but these camels were almost constantly in use hauling firewood from the Carson River to Virginia City.

The Bactrians also had one distinct advantage over the dromedaries in that their exceptionally long brown hair was in great demand for weaving camel-hair bridles, ropes and the like. Earlier in 1864 the Gold Hill *News* had reported on some camels in Virginia City which were being "plucked" of their long winter hair, and since one camel could produce up to ten pounds of long silky hair it was still one additional way of earning revenue.

> *When the Army's camels were first being purchased in the Mid-East, some difficulty was encountered in loading them onto the storeship Supply. Finally a ramp was constructed to a small scow, the animals were loaded aboard it, then transferred in mid-harbor to the storeship.*

On June 30, 1877, more than two years after camels had been banned by the Nevada Legislature, Harper's Weekly finally got around to featuring an illustration of a camel train in this state.

The Chevaliers were very successfully breeding and raising camels on their Carson River ranch. The animals thrived on the sparse desert vegetation by eating, as one editor put it, "willows and greasewood and sage brush and obsolete playing cards and old cast-off clothes." They adapted quite well to the seasonal climate changes, but their soft feet had to be protected from the rocky terrain. Occasionally leather "shoes" were laced over the animals' feet when they had to trod exceptionally stony ground.

By October 1864 — the month Nevada became a state — some camels were being placed on sale. Lammon & Palmer conducted an auction in Virginia City that month, but the prices ranged ridiculously low — $100 to $225 per animal.

Samuel McLeneghan brought his remaining camels to Nevada from California in 1865, but there was very little profit to be made with them while competing with the established freight outfits. He and LaFlamme and most of the camels then headed south to Arizona. Soon after their arrival at

Fort Yuma McLeneghan died, and his camels were thereafter dispersed in various southwestern mining camps.

That same year, while the first buildings at the Mormon settlement of Callville, Nevada were under construction, a group of local Indians was sent downriver to watch for the arrival of a steamboat bearing supplies. Not knowing what a steamboat looked like, one Indian runner soon returned to camp breathless, claiming that he had found "steamboat tracks" in the sand. That of course stopped all work on the buildings and the curious Mormons followed the Indian back to determine what he had really found. The tracks were spotted and trailed for a time until a solitary camel appeared in the desert. He was captured and his owner, John Young of Salt Lake City, was notified, providing a good laugh at the expense of the Indians.

In 1865 the Overland Camel Company was incorporated in New York City to utilize the animals between the Mississippi River and the Pacific Ocean, although this firm never actually operated. At the same time camel use in Nevada declined although they hauled great amounts of freight from Virginia City to Austin throughout 1866. The following year some of the Chevalier camels transported coal to Virginia City and freight to the new camp of Belmont, but their novelty soon wore thin.

Ever since the first group of Army horses and mules was stampeded in Texas in 1856, camels consistently frightened other animals. Real trouble occurred in October 1868 when a carriage driven along the Carson River road was stampeded by grazing camels. No harm came to the badly shaken passengers but since Judge A. W. Baldwin and General Thomas H. Williams were passengers in the carriage, the press began a campaign to get rid of the offensive animals.

Built by George Leslie, the small stone barn in Dayton was used by McLeneghan and LaFlamme to stable their camels. Although it was only used in this manner for a very brief period, the building is still known as the old "camel barn."

Many have stated that Virginia City once passed an ordinance prohibiting their use within the city limits during daylight hours, but a thorough search of both city and county ordinances does not confirm this. Only section four of the 1868 city ordinances gives a clue: "No person shall ride or drive through any street or highway within the limits of the city ... in such a manner as to endanger the public safety."

As Alf Doten in his famous diary mentioned in 1868, camels "are never allowed to pass public roads & streets in daytime on acc't of frightening animals..." The city fathers probably used section four to keep camels out of town.

By 1870 the Chevaliers' herd had grown to 26 camels, all but two of which were born and raised in Nevada. They were still in use occasionally to haul salt from the vicinity of Sand Springs to the Comstock reduction mills along the Carson River, and in 1872 the *Territorial Enterprise* reported that one train hauled hay from the Carson River to Adams' hay-yard on North D Street. The following year they still brought freight to Virginia City, stabling at the Clipper Gap wagon yard when in town, but the campaign against them steadily mounted.

The Carson *Daily Appeal* stated, "Appearing suddenly and without warning in the road, he causes the heart of horse and mule and ass to quake with supernatural and superstitious fear." To make matters worse, the camels were exceedingly tame, prompting "a familiarity for men and women and buggies and horses and mules and asses and jerk-water wagons which is almost unbearable."

On January 20, 1875, the situation climaxed. Assemblyman Hugh Carling of Lyon County, where most camels were kept, introduced a bill in the state legislature to ban camels and dromedaries from the public

CHAP. XII.—An Act to prohibit camels and dromedaries from running at large on or about the public highways of the State of Nevada.

[Approved February 9, 1875.]

The People of the State of Nevada, represented in Senate and Assembly, do enact as follows:

SECTION 1. From and after the passage of this Act it shall be unlawful for the owner or owners of any camel or camels, dromedary or dromedaries, to permit them to run at large on or about the public roads or highways of this State.

SEC. 2. If any owner or owners of any camel or camels, dromedary or dromedaries shall, knowingly and willfully, permit any violation of this Act, he or they shall be deemed guilty of a misdemeanor, and shall be arrested, on complaint of any person feeling aggrieved; and when convicted, before any Justice of the Peace, he or they shall be punished by a fine not less than twenty-five (25) or more than one hundred (100) dollars, ...ment not less than ten or more than thirty days, ... imprisonment.

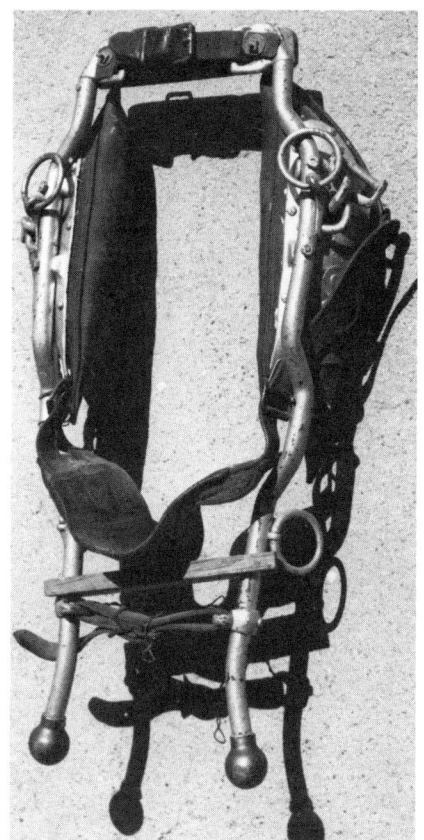

The only known American made camel saddle of the 19th century is a skimpy double-pommel rig obviously constructed for a Bactrian camel. The tree is cast steel, fully covered in leather, and is marked "J. T. Morgan, Maker, Boise, I.T." It was likely built for the Bactrians which Frank Laumeister used in Canada and later in Montana before taking them to Arizona in 1872.

highways of Nevada. Virginia City's *Territorial Enterprise*, which had previously been outraged by the danger these animals posed, suddenly reversed itself. "Members should remember that these animals were brought here originally at great expense by the government; they thrive well in the desert; they are useful as pack animals; the man or men who own them have property rights. All these things must be considered. To turn them off the roads is to destroy their usefulness." The Carson *Daily Appeal*, though, stipulated the many reasons why the animals should be abated.

In the Assembly the bill to ban camels caused much humor although it passed on February 3. In the Senate it was first suggested that the hippopotamus be included with camels, then Senator McClinton pointedly asked if those long eared mules did not occasionally scare the camels and dromedaries? After the laughter faded the Senate also approved the measure on February 5. It became law on February 9, thus effectively doing away with the use of camels to haul freight in Nevada.

Naturally Virginia City continued to live up to its reputation of doing things its own way, allowing at least limited use of camels. The nation's centennial saw Comstock residents determined to have their own unique celebration. Some built a bonfire on the peak of Sun Mountain which would be visible for more than 200 miles. A camel train was hired, probably one of the Chevaliers' strings, and for several days preceeding July 4 they

plodded up the steep mountainside carrying huge loads of firewood. By the time the wood was ready to be lit, the pile was 16 feet tall; everything was carried to the 7,864-foot summit by camels.

The local chapter of the Horrible Club, a group quite similiar to today's Order of E. Clampus Vitus, obtained special permission by the Board of Aldermen to use camels in the Independence Day parade as well. At the last minute common sense prevailed, and the camels deferred to the many horses in the parade.

At least two Nevada camels may have been shipped east for exhibition at the huge Centennial Exposition at Philadelphia, after which they were to be donated to the Philadelphia zoo. Though their role in the exposition is uncertain, Bancroft's *History of Nevada* does state that "a part of the herd was disposed of to the Philadelphia zoological gardens."

As late as October 31, 1876 the *Territorial Enterprise* reported a 20-camel train arriving in town laden with firewood, but the strange beasts thereafter faded from the scene. The remaining few were put out to pasture, although the cost of their upkeep eventually moved their owners to turn them loose in the Nevada deserts.

It is reported that Frank Laumeister, who owned the camel pack trains which operated in the Cariboo region of British Columbia, brought his camels to Elko, Nevada when he purchased the hot springs spa located there. He may also have taken them to Pioche, Nevada in 1872, but neither locale ever confirmed their arrival. It is probable that he did ship them to Yuma, Arizona late in 1872, thus perhaps passing through Nevada enroute, but this too has not been verified.

This Southwestern camel train has been the subject of speculation as to where the photo was taken. The extremely large number of camels in one train and the stone-covered flat which they are traversing suggests Arizona. Note the leather "shoes" the animals are wearing to protect their feet from the sharp stones. A few dromedaries also appear to be mixed in with the Bactrians, further disputing the idea that this could be a Nevada train, as the two species were used separately in this state. The train likely dates from the 1880's when the Southern Pacific RR used camels in Arizona to haul freight.

The Chevaliers, who had grown attached to their animals, refused to abandon them in the sage wastes. In the spring of 1877 they took their ever-growing herd, now numbering 41 head, and started south toward Arizona. The group roughly followed the route of present U.S. 395, losing five animals along the way, arriving in Fort Yuma in mid-March. Sadly, there were no takers for their services, so the camels were then set free in the Arizona desert.

The Southern Pacific Railroad in Arizona reportedly used about 400 camels in the early 1880's, principally for hauling freight to outlying areas. Undoubtedly many of these were animals which had once belonged to Esche, McLeneghan, Laumeister and the Chevaliers. When the railroad decided to sell them in 1884, the Carson City *Morning Appeal* announced that the 400 camels had been purchased by John Shirley for shipment to his huge sheep ranch in the Australian outback.

By 1899 so few camels remained in Nevada that the 1875 law banning their use was finally repealed. Not all had been taken to Arizona though, and beasts thrived in the Nevada deserts for a few decades. In 1905 the Goldfield *News* reported that someone had spotted a herd of 16 camels at a spring near Silver Bow, and as late as 1936 a band of 20 camels was supposedly living near Penelas.

Eventually they all perished, either from the elements or predators, until all that remain are the legends. A large red camel supposedly jaunts the steep slopes of Sun Mountain above Virginia City and is only visible on nights of a full moon. Another legend has a ghost camel train roaming the various Nevada salt flats with a skeleton lashed to one of the animals.

Finally even the legends began to pale until Bob Richards, editor of the *Territorial Enterprise* in Virginia City, hit upon a novel idea in 1959. Following an age-old Nevada newspaper tradition of inventing news when the real article was in short supply, he wrote a brief piece announcing the results of the town's annual camel race. Actually there had been no race, and the item generated little comment locally as the area's residents were well accustomed to the editor's flights of fancy.

The author (opposite page) competed for seven years as a camel jockey, and was also a participant in ostrich races.

A well balanced rider can release a hand from the saddle to use a whip, as this jockey is doing, but a sudden turn by the animal very often results in a fall.

The San Francisco *Chronicle* took notice, however, and when another article appeared in the *Enterprise* the following year announcing the upcoming running of the fictional race, the *Chronicle* hired a camel and a jockey to compete. Both the Phoenix *Gazette* and the Indio, California, Chamber of Commerce then challenged the *Chronicle*. Suddenly the fictional race was fast becoming a reality. Camels were provided by a San Francisco zoo, trucked to Virginia City, and the *Chronicle's* own entry, ridden by movie director John Huston, captured the trophy in 1960.

ACKNOWLEDGEMENTS: The author thanks the following for their assistance with this work: Eslie Cann and Lee Mortensen, Reno; Walter Daniels, Virginia City; and Marsh and Frank Fey of Reno whose race sponsorship enabled me to acquire firsthand experience with camels.

PHOTO CREDITS: Nevada Historical Society, 3, 4, 8, 9, 10, 12, 15, 19; California Historical Society, 6; John Zalac of Carson City, 16; Dan Heath of Virginia City, front cover, map on rear cover, 23; Roscoe Willson Collection, Arizona Historical Foundation, 24; Washoe County Library, 21.

With nothing more than an editor's fanciful newspaper article to instigate it, modern camel racing began in Virginia City in 1960. The event has always been dangerous — a camel's temper is a legendary topic in the Mid-East. A swift-running camel at full speed has a marvelous gait. Here Marilyn Newton attempts to stay aboard her mount while Bill Curl and Nevada Smith try to get it to the starting line. The animal's loose skin, flexible hump, and ability to make rapid turns make staying on a difficult task.

Ostrich Races

Ostrich racing was only introduced into Nevada during the 1962 camel races in Virginia City, but these animals also have an historical precedent in this state. In 1879 Theodore Glancy purchased a ranch southwest of Bismark Peak in the Pine Nut Range southeast of Carson City. His intention was to use ostriches as pack animals to "transport provisions and other parcels" and to periodically sell their feathers.

At first he attempted to hatch ostrich eggs by solar heat but this experiment failed. Glancy then obtained a pair of ostriches in 1881 from which he eventually raised ten others. However, his grand idea of an "ostrich pack train" fell by the wayside and nothing further was heard of this experiment.

The race proved to be such a success that it became an annual event, though one year, 1976, the race was shifted out of state to Sacramento. Beginning in 1962 ostrich racing was added to the Virginia City show, then the following year the course was moved from B to C Street, the town's main thoroughfare. Since this proved unsuitable, the site was soon changed to E Street, where the races are still held.

Problems plagued the early races, which the *Enterprise* in 1966 called "punk troubles and hoodlumism," even though that year's event made a profit of $1,524.72. Because of the problems the 1967 races were moved to Reno. This caused such a void in the Comstock's activities for the year that the event was happily reinstituted in 1968, when for the first time the race dates were moved from August to September.

Riders who competed in the races returned in succeeding years to compete again. A loose organization developed which in 1972 became the International Order of Camel Jockeys (I.O.C.J.), and for ten years it provided most of the riders for the race's sponsors. When the band of camels rented annually from a southern California wild animal farm was due to be dispersed in the late 1970's, a separate organization was formed to acquire and maintain this large herd of Arabian camels. Known as the Association for the Protection and Procreation of Indigenous Animals — Camels (A.P.P.I.A.), this group maintains most of its herd in California, making animals available for special shows and races.

In early 1982 three of the A.P.P.I.A.'s camels helped recreate the 1861 survey of the California-Nevada border. Beginning on February 13 the group retraced the steps of the original surveyors, with the 54-day trek once again reestablishing the camel's suitability to perform in almost any terrain or climate.

Early in 1983 the Nevada camel racing scene took on new dimensions when it was decided to hold two races that year, both on the same weekend, in Reno and Virginia City. A dispute between the Virginia City Chamber of Commerce and the I.O.C.J. established two races instead of the previous one, which may benefit both Virginia City and the newly popular sport of camel racing.

After an absence of some eighty years, the camel races brought a return of the hump-backed animals to the Silver State. Broken bones, concussions and various injuries are not uncommon, though the riders do an admirable job of turning a normal camel race into a parody of a Mid-Eastern rodeo.

In Nevada three historic monuments commemorate the early camels: a State Parks plaque at the southern tip of Nevada recalls the federal "Camel Corps," a pyramid-shaped monument in Virginia City honors camels employed on the Comstock, and a marker at Dayton memorializes the still-standing camel barn used by McLeneghan. Besides these, the annual camel race is a modern reminder of the time when camels were part of the West's transportation industry, and their presence was instrumental in the writing of some of the strangest traffic laws ever enacted in Nevada.

A B C's of Camels

Arabian camel (dromedary), *Camelus dromedarius*, has one hump.
Bactrian camel, *Camelus bactrianus*, has two humps.
Earliest predecessor, *Protylopus*, originated in North America millions of years ago. Evolved into *Procamelus*, migrated over land bridge to Asia, died out in W. hemisphere, evolved into modern animals in Asia.
Survival features: extra 15 gallons of water is stored in stomach; hump carries fat to be used for emergency subsistence.
Camel first domesticated during biblical times. First used in warfare by Midianites in the time of Gideon. Endurance records: one camel and rider sped from Cairo to Antioch, 560 miles, in 5½ days; Mehemet Ali rode from Suez to Cairo, 84 miles, in 12 hours; a racing dromedary covered the 115 miles from Esneh to Keneh in 11 hours; and British Col. Chesney rode his camel 960 miles in 19 days with no food but what the animal could forage.
Normal pack weights: Barbary camels carry 550-600 pounds while covering 40 miles a day; near Mt. Sinai camels are known to pack some 780 pounds each for 30-45 miles a day over stony ground; and Syrian camels often carry two bales weighing a total of 1,000 pounds.